TAROT SPREADS FOR LOVE

REAL WORLD TAROT BOOKS

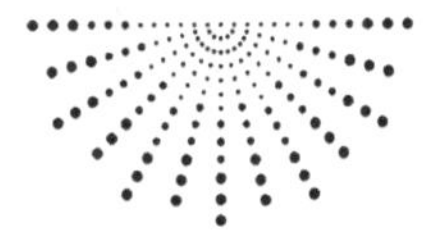

KAT ELMWOOD

SEEKERS GROVE PRESS

CONTENTS

TAROT SPREADS FOR SELF-LOVE

FRIENDSHIP

PARENT AND CHILD LOVE

DIVINE LOVE

INTRODUCTION

Love is all we need. Love is in the air. Love makes the world go round. Love is a battlefield. Love lifts us up where we belong. Love, love, love...

Love saturates us like rain, soaking the earth, seeping into the deepest corners of our being, nourishing us, sometimes drowning us.

Love's warmth courses through our veins, creating a tapestry of shared moments and intertwined destinies. When it breaks, the disturbance of that warmth feels like it could destroy us down to our very cells.

Love colors our lives in every shade of light and dark. It gives us meaning; it dissolves barriers, forges and breaks bonds.

Love, in all its forms, is our universe.

There is no wonder that matters of the heart are one of the most common reasons people come to tarot looking for answers.

Querents come to the cards looking for advice on what to do when love goes wrong. We ask the cards for insight into our lover's minds. We want yes or no answers of whether to pursue certain relationships, or whether to walk away from them. We want the cards to teach us how to get more love into our lives, and we want the cards to teach us how to heal when love leaves.

Tarot traditions are infused with love. Love connects to us at every level of our consciousness, and tarot speaks to all these levels too. It's a perfect match! Whether we're talking about romantic love, lust and passion, the love of a parent, the love of a child, friendship, a relationship with the divine, or the love of one's self, themes of love can be explored with tarot from its deepest roots to its highest spiritual aspirations. The spreads in this book explore these nuances of love and relationships and more.

These spreads have been designed around some of the most common situations, problems, and questions we have surrounding love. The book is divided into five chapters of different types of love. Romantic love, the most detailed chapter, covers matters of romantic unions. These might be questions about people we are already in relationships with, people who we long to be in relationships with, or people we used to be in relationships with. Light and dark romantic issues are explored in these spreads. We also look at self-love and how we can develop more love for ourselves.

Friendship is an important theme many of us overlook when thinking about love. In this chapter, we look at our current friendships, making new friends, and repairing bonds with old friends. Parent and child love might be the most foundational love we all experience. Everything we go through in life is colored by our attachment to our parental caregivers, even as adults. The spreads in this chapter look at how to examine the connection between a parent and child, how parents can grow into love and help their children do the same. We also talk about how to repair fractured parental bonds, and how love can flow holistically through a family unit. In the final chapter, we look at divine love. This is the love you experience in a relationship with a divine spirit. You might call this God, or Source, or Holy Spirit, or Universe, or many other names. It doesn't matter what religion or spiritual path you follow, the spreads in this chapter can all be used to deepen your love toward your version of the divine spirit, growing in faith, looking for evidence of ways your divine spirit loves you back.

Some spreads in this book are accompanied by diagrams to guide you in your card layout. These spreads have been designed with symbolic intention. Following the patterns can add a sense of ritual and creative connection to your readings. However, in every spread, the suggested layouts are presented as optional guides. You can and should always lay your spreads as it feels best to you. If that's an intricate pattern suggested here or made up by you, then go for it. If you prefer your cards in a straight line or any other simple arrangement, then embrace that, too.

Some spreads have brief explanations for what each card signifies within the layout. Other card positions are simply labeled without further explanation. Use these labels to create your own intuitive meanings for what any card should signify to you.

Similarly, some spreads are introduced through brief discussions of the themes at hand. These discussions are always opinion, offered to guide your understanding of the intention used to develop each spread. You might have your own opinions and should proceed at every stage as your own guide. Some of these discussions also include instructions on laying the spread. Again, consider these optional suggestions.

HOW TO READ TAROT FOR LOVE

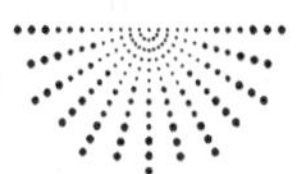

Whether you're seeking answers and guidance for a romantic love, self-love, a friendship, the love of a family member, or the love of your divine spirit, the process is the same.

Hold your feelings, your questions, your musings in your mind as you shuffle the cards. You might like to choose a deck specifically representative of your feelings or of your relationship, or love in general. See my list of The Best Tarot Decks For Love on Tarot Junction for a selection of decks well suited to love readings (https://www.tarotjunction.-com/best-tarot-decks-for-love/).

You might have a pre-designed spread already in mind, such as those in this book, or you can lay the cards intuitively. As with most things in tarot, whatever feels right for you in the moment is the best way to proceed.

Whether tarot can literally see the future and predict what will happen in your love life is a matter of personal belief. But what tarot can absolutely do is provide insight into what you are thinking or feeling about your past, present, and future relationships, and prompt guidance from your inner knowing of what is best for you at this time.

SHOULD I READ INTUITIVELY OR USE TRADITIONAL MEANINGS?

An intuitive reading is a conversation between you and your cards, your heart and mind, with using tarot's symbolic language that speaks directly to your subconscious. Intuitive reading of tarot for matters of the heart can be more appropriate when tapping into your inner guidance.

However, while intuitive reading is wonderful, often we are so lost in the mire of our feelings, conflicting needs, and paradoxical thoughts–after all, love makes us crazy sometimes–it can be a clarifying comfort to lean on the traditions of the cards and let those established meanings speak to us directly.

You can always combine a mixture of the two approaches into any reading. This is my preferred way of reading tarot on any topic.

Read the cards intuitively first. Note down your primary thoughts, reactions, and or visions. I like to do this in my journal, but you might prefer more spontaneous observations. When I have read the spread intuitively, I then compare and contrast my intuitive reading with the traditional meanings of the cards.

And yes, it's perfectly okay to consult your tarot books and any tarot resources for meanings of the traditional cards if you haven't memorized them yet (or never plan to!).

This book does not go into detail on how to actually perform a tarot reading or explain the different components of a deck. If you are new to tarot and need further guidance in understanding how tarot works before exploring these love spreads, please see my introductory books, *Tarot For Beginners* and *Tarot Meanings*.

A NOTE ON GENDER IN TAROT

Within the standard modern decks, mostly inspired by the Rider-Waite-Smith tradition, many cards carry gendered titles such as Emperor, Priestess, Empress, or Hanged Man, as well as Kings and Queens. Additionally, certain cards traditionally depict gendered representations, for example, The Fool and The Chariot often show a male figure, while Strength and The Star frequent a female representation. There are also cards that traditionally depict a male and female pairing, such as The Lovers and The Devil.

Not all decks have these binary gendered characters. Some depict all men, some are entirely women, some have trans and queer figures, some decks are entirely gender neutral. Some do not show people at all.

When reading for matters of love, it might be tempting to see your paramour in these figured cards as the person themselves. For example, if you are a heterosexual cis woman, you might see any man depicted on a card as your love interest. There's nothing wrong with this interpretation if that's what feels best to you.

However, gender in the cards does not actually refer to physical distinctions between scientifically classified male and scientifically classified female. The energies represented in these cards more closely refer to the broader physical and spiritual energy spectrum commonly termed as masculine and feminine. In Jungian psychology, this is the archetype of the animus and anima.

The masculine energy, animus, aligns with the physical and earthly outer energies. The feminine energies, anima, are associated with the emotional, psychological, and spiritual realms of internal energies. It's crucial to note that these energies can simultaneously coexist within the same card, as well as in the same person. For instance, The Hermit card typically portrays a masculine figure, yet its essence delves into a feminine energy, symbolizing a retreat for emotional, psychological pondering, healing, and replenishment.

Throughout this book, and all books in my tarot series, I use traditionally gendered pronouns based on the representations in the decks I am using for demonstration. For instance, when discussing RWS Hermit, I will use "he." However, please understand that this discussion revolves around energy and personality, operating within a cyclical spectrum. "He" is referring to the animus; "she" the anima. If I use a gendered pronoun and it does not align with your identity or beliefs, please recognize it as a shorthand for energy not reference to scientifically classified sex at birth or binary gender identifications. Please apply your preferred pronouns and labels as you like and carry them into your readings.

TAROT CARDS ASSOCIATED WITH LOVE

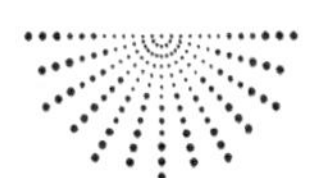

Is there a card in the tarot that *couldn't* be associated with matters of the heart, if read with the right perspective? While love and relationships can infuse the narrative of any deck, there are certain cards and groupings that speak more directly to matters of love.

CARD GROUPINGS

Major Arcana Cards

Since the Major Arcana cards connect to the bigger, fateful events in our lives, drawing a Major Arcana card in a love reading foretells significant moments. This might be the earth shifting experiences of falling for a lover, becoming a parent, or losing any loved one, or any major life moment that is directly shared with a partner.

Forces beyond our earthly control may be at play in the Major Arcana and lead us to think of matters of pre-written fate and destiny. If you're looking for a card that represents the one true love you are fated to be with (if you believe in The One), then the Major cards are probably where you will find this person.

. . .

Minor Arcana Cards

The Minor cards are our day-to-day moments. Minor Arcana cards typically delve into the more nuanced feelings, little moments, minor conflicts, or conversations. These might also refer to things you do with your partner in general life rather than the overall relationship itself.

Each card in the Minor suits has its special relevancy depending on its number. Some of these can be especially relevant to love spreads. For example, two cards represent unions; five cards represent turning points; three cards represent group dynamics; and ten cards represent outcomes. When an Ace card appears in a tarot reading, we are traditionally looking at the entire spirit of the suit condensed into that card in a raw form. See the discussion on the Ace of Cups below.

Cups

The suite of Cups is all about the feminine energy of emotion and inner consciousness. Cups deal in matters of relationships, intuition, creativity and feelings, so they are prime high energy cards for any reading about love.

The Cups are associated with the water element. It's flowing, ever moving, and life giving, a power just as gentle as it is torrential and terrible. Just like love. When water stops moving, it grows stagnant, just as when our emotional states stop moving.

Swords

We traditionally think of the Swords cards as masculine representations of action and outward power. Conflict comes heavily into the realm of Swords. As such, when we see a Sword card in a love reading, it might refer to actions one needs to take in a relationship, whether that's positive or negative. It might also refer to direct conflict within love, perhaps even the breakdown of a partnership.

It need not be always bleak to see a Sword card in a love spread. The Swords here might also refer to matters of tough love (common in family or friendship dynamics). Swords are also associated with matters of communication, a critical factor in any relationship.

The Court Figures

The Court cards are the four figures at the end of each Minor Arcana suit. They are Page, Knight, Queen, and King.

Some think of these figures as being personality traits of the suit, evolving progressively through these Court's ranks. The Court cards, even though they appear as figures, need not represent specific people in the querent's life. They might, of course, but they could also be all about personality traits, or philosophies.

Pages

The most youthful member of the Court, the Page approaches the suit's energies with curiosity and playfulness. While still in the process of growing into the nature of their suit, Pages engage with the suit's qualities with a fresh mind devoid of judgements. The Page might be the person newly in love, full of idyllic notions and visions of happily ever after, before real life comes to complicate matters.

Knights

Knights are keen, powerful, and smart characters. Despite these strengths, Knights are still youthful. Knights are noble and strong, they do good work, and are capable of great things, but they are prone to recklessness and imbalance without proper guidance. In matters of love, the Knight is passion without much reason, all heart and not a lot of mind. See the Knight of Cups below.

Queens

Queens are the ultimate feminine energy of their suits. They are all about creation and inward reflection and wisdom, and take their power from an inner source. Queens are the wise women of love, the grand matriarchs of the realms of the heart. She has had her hardships, her grand passions and now offers all the wisdom tempered from all kinds of life experiences to the querent.

Kings

Kings are the ultimate masculine energies of their suits. Kings are outwardly focused, wise, and strong. Kings might refer to paternal or dominant figures, protectors, leaders, and providers.

INDIVIDUAL CARDS

The Lovers

For obvious reasons, The Lovers card is most directly associated with love and relationships. In Rider-Waite-Smith traditions, The Lovers card traditionally depicts a couple, usually naked, standing in a lush garden (connoting the Biblical Eden), watched over by a divine angelic figure. A mountain, symbolizing hardships to conquer, looms between them.

Traditionally, The Lovers card need not specifically refer to a relationship or partnership. This card is about a choice between two paths, and a profound connection between two forces. These choices need to provide harmony, aligning the yearnings of the heart with the values of the higher self.

In love readings, we are most likely going to read this as choices we make in relationships; perhaps a choice of partners, or perhaps even a choice we might have to make between a partner and our self. It is about emotional and spiritual alignment, ensuring our relationships serve us wholly as physical beings.

Two of Cups

This card is traditionally associated with partnership and mutually beneficial unions. It can represent the beginnings of a romantic relationship, or the deepening of bonds of any loving nature.

Ten of Cups

As a ten card, the Ten of Cups signifies fulfillment. In relationship terms, this would be emotional contentment and blissful harmony within the union, be that a romantic relationship or any other bond. The Ten of Cups traditionally has strong associations with familial togetherness.

Ace of Cups

This card is associated with new beginnings in matters of emotions. It can indicate the start of a new romantic connection, or the deepening of existing feelings. As with all Ace cards, the Ace of Cups is the height of emotion. It's a passionate primal energy.

Knight of Cups

The Knight of Cups is a romantic and charming individual. Think of the quintessential knight of chivalric tales, such as the Knights of the Round Table. It can represent someone who is emotionally expressive and may bring messages of new love or proposals. The Knight can come with a warning, though. As Knights are not fully mature cards, your passionate Knight might not be acting with the full benefit of learned wisdom.

Four of Wands

The Four of Wands is traditionally associated with celebration and harmony. In a romantic context, the Four of Wands might speak to the joy and stability within a relationship. As a Wands card, this is about manifestation, so it might be speaking to the work we need to do within a relationship to reach these contented states.

The Tower

The Tower card is often considered the most negative card in tarot tradition. It is about destruction and upheaval, cataclysmic events that shake our very foundations. Of course, it's difficult to see these things as positive when they are occurring. However, if we look at the negatives of The Tower card within the whole narrative of the tarot, we see that this destruction follows a building up of challenging energy that, once erupted, results in renewal, change, and growth for the better.

In a love and relationships tarot reading, The Tower most obviously means a breakup, but it might also refer to another disruptive and transformative turning point.

The appearance of The Tower in spread, particularly when dealing with matters of the heart, can be frightening if viewed with pessimism, but remember that while initially disruptive and potentially hurtful, the Tower's impact is ultimately constructive allowing for the emergence of a stronger, more genuine connection with your partner, with a new partner, or with yourself.

The Star

The Star is a card of hope, renewal and inspiration, and is typically a delightful and positive card. In the narrative of the Major Arcana, the Star card follows the Tower, the ultimate symbol of destruction. So the hope embodied in this card is the light following dark, the renewal at the end of the struggle. The Star is a card of healing and replenishment.

This is a strong feminine card, and as such, we might consider that this hope and renewal comes from within ourselves, not from others. But since it also speaks to celestial notions, we might also infer that we are supported in our healing by universal forces. Be open to the love of the universe and let it guide you toward blessings of happiness.

The Sun

The Sun card in a love tarot reading radiates positivity and joy, symbolizing warmth and fulfillment. When we follow the narrative of the previous three cards within the Arcana, we see the destruction from The Tower leading to the inner renewal and then internal searching of The Star and The Moon, culminating in the joyous warmth of The Sun.

When reading for love, The Sun heralds clarity, honesty, and a deep emotional connection between partners or the self. It embodies vitality, encouraging us to embrace our genuine selves within a nurturing partnership, or within our graceful autonomy.

TAROT SPREADS FOR ROMANTIC LOVE

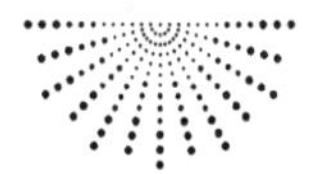

SINGLE CARD DRAWS FOR ROMANTIC LOVE

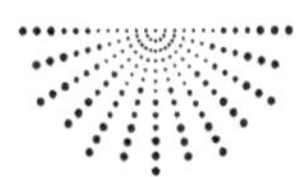

The single card draw is a quick yet powerful tool in reading tarot.

It can be used to gain an overview of your situation when you don't have time or energy for a more involved spread. It can also be used to get an overview of the situation when you're not entirely sure what you're questioning, what you're feeling, or your general position in your romantic situation. In this sense, a single card draw can give you a kind of tone note for your love life.

INTUITIVE SINGLE CARD DRAW

It can be useful sometimes to approach a single card draw with an entirely intuitive position, letting the card, your subconscious, and your feelings have an off-the-cuff conversation.

To do this, simply shuffle the deck and then draw a card. You don't have to think about the traditional meanings of the cards if you don't want to. Just rely on the story that you infer from the card's title, art, visual symbolism, and anything else that particularly stands out.

You can then intuitively decide what this card means about your love life at that moment. You can decide if it's an overview card, or if it means something specific. You might also choose to use it as a prompt for further questioning, following which you can draw more cards or start a detailed reading in a formal spread.

DIRECTED SINGLE CARD DRAWS

For a little more direction in your single card draws, here are some suggestions to inspire your readings in certain directions. With these prompts, you can read the card intuitively, traditionally or, a combination of both intuition and tradition.

- Overall energy of your love life.
- A significator card for your current partner.
- Significant a card for a prospective partner.
- Overview tone on how to best approach a break-up.
- Tone on how to heal after a break-up.
- A particular theme of your love life in your past.
- A particular theme of your current love life.
- An area of your life you need to focus on in order to feel secure in your romantic situations, whether you are single or partnered.
- The underlying themes of tensions in a relationship.
- The underlying strengths of a relationship.
- Areas where communication is breaking down.
- Areas where attachment styles might be different between you and your partner, which could cause conflicts.

- Any Yes No binary types of questions you have
  about specific concerns, positive or negative,
  within your love life.

THREE CARD SPREADS FOR ROMANTIC RELATIONSHIPS

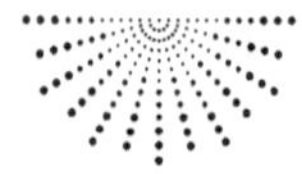

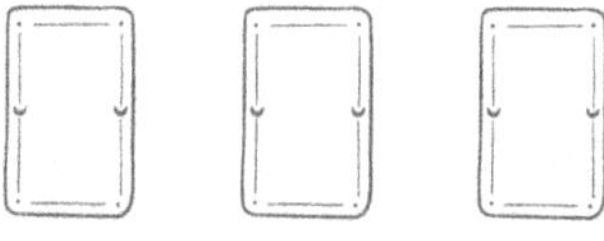

THREE CARD SPREADS

Like single card draws, three cards spreads can be simple, quick, and incredibly powerful. A three card spread can provide a brief insight into an overall situation, alternatively the individual three cards might represent different aspects of your situation. In these kinds of spreads, your answers are usually in the relationships between the cards, not so much the individual card meanings.

RELATIONSHIP POTENTIAL

1. You.
2. The other.
3. Your potential together.

RELATIONSHIP OVERVIEW

1. You.
2. Them.
3. The relationship.

WHAT YOU BOTH WANT

1. What you want.
2. What they want.
3. The compromise.

WHAT YOU BOTH NEED

1. What you need.
2. What they need.
3. The compromise.

PAST, PRESENT, FUTURE

1. Your past experiences in romance.
2. Your current relationship.
3. Your future, either together or yours alone.

PUSH AND PULL

1. What's bringing you together?
2. What's pushing you apart?
3. Compromises.

CHOOSING

1. Prospective partner one.
2. Prospective partner two.
3. Your highest need in a partner.

ROLES

1. Your role.
2. Their role.
3. Overall dynamics.

You can build on any of these spreads, or any three card spread you devise on your own, by adding further clarifier cards where you feel it's necessary.

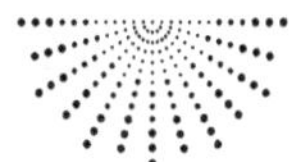

RELATIONSHIP OVERVIEW

1. You Presently
This card shows your feelings and thoughts in the relationship.

2. Your Partner Presently
Reveals your partner's feelings and thoughts.

3. Points of connection

Elements that draw you together.

4. Challenges

Elements that create conflict and tension.

5. Your Strengths

Your personal strengths that can help navigate challenges.

6. Their Strengths

Your partner's strengths that can help navigate challenges.

7. External Forces

Shows external factors affecting your relationship.

8. Positives

All the good things about being together.

9. Hopes and Desires

What you both want and need.

10. Future Path

Where the relationship is headed.

THE CRUSH

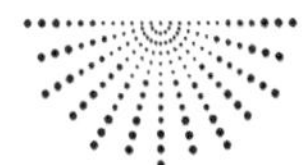

This spread can be a fun way to think of future potential partners when you have met someone, and are considering pursuing a relationship with them.

The Crush spread is not about mind-reading the other person to see if they like you. It's about you considering what insights you have already on how the other person thinks and feels.

1. Your feelings about a prospective relationship in general.
2. Your feelings about a prospective relationship with this person specifically.
3. Your prospective partner's feelings about the relationship.
4. The relationship energy.
5. Best point to bring you together.
6. Potential challenges
7. Overall potential of the union.

THE CRUSH

LOVE IN THE FUTURE

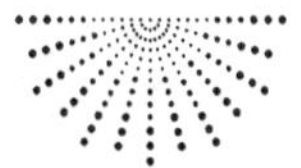

LOVE IN THE FUTURE

This spread looks towards the future to figure out what you want from a relationship, and how you feel about your current positions in love.

While Love In The Future hints at the divination associations of tarot, this spread it's not about literally seeing the future. It's about life design, figuring out who you are and what you want in the present, and how you might use that to shape your future.

1. Current Self

Your present emotional state.

2. Ideal Future Partner

Qualities and energies your future partner would ideally possess.

3. Meet Cute

Insights into how you might best meet your potential new partner.

4. Personal Obstacles

Your personal challenges that may hinder your path to love.

5. Hidden Desires

What you unconsciously desire in a relationship.

6. Wise Guidance

Universal wisdom for bringing love into your life.

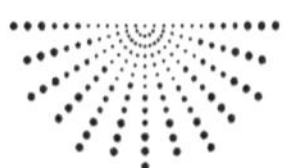

QUESTIONING A CHALLENGING RELATIONSHIP

1. Your Emotions

Your current feelings and thoughts regarding the union.

2. Their Emotions

Your partner's emotions and thoughts.

3. Emotional Harmony
The emotional and spiritual balances between both of you.

4. Hurdles
Core challenges that are in the way of reaching this harmony.

5. Renewal
The relationship's potential for healing.

ARE WE GOOD TOGETHER?

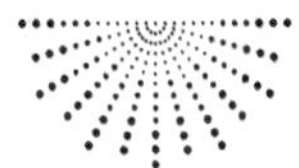

1. Current Connection
Present state of your relationship.

2. Obstacles
Hindrances to the connection.

3. Strengths
Highlights the positive elements strengthening your bond.

4. Core Bond
The core elements that hold you together.

5. Communication
How effectively you communicate with each other.

7. Outcome
The potential long-term outcome of your connection.

PERSONAL RESPONSIBILITY WITHIN A RELATIONSHIP - DUAL SPREAD

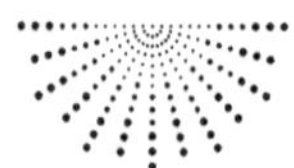

This spread focuses on an individual's role within a relationship. It's beneficial to explore these themes with your partner, where each of you pulls a card for each of these positions. When you have both completed your double spread, read the separate spreads as individuals, and then look for the relationship between the spreads.

If you choose to do the spread as a dual spread, it can be a lovely idea to draw an additional card and place it between your two spreads. This card represents the spirit of the relationship, an amalgam of your combined selves.

If your partner is not into tarot, and can't be convinced to participate in this dual spread, you can still benefit from its insights by performing it on yourself.

Each partner draws cards for the following:

1. What do I want from a relationship?
2. What do I need most in my overall life?
3. The strengths of our union.
4. The weaknesses of the union.

5. Best way to address our core challenges.
6. My individual role in challenges.
7. Best steps toward personal growth within the
   union.
8. Optional relationship Signifier that combines both
   sides, if laying as a dual spread.

HIGHER WISDOM PARTNER CHECK-IN - DUAL SPREAD

Performing this spread with your partner can be a romantic way to check-in with each other, either as a one-off event, or something to come back to time and time again to keep the relationship on track.

If you prefer to do this spread as a check-in with yourself and not involve your partner, that can also work as a wonderful opportunity for self-exploration.

1. Message of higher wisdom.
2. Perception of the self in relationship to the higher wisdom.
3. Perception of the partner in relationship to the higher wisdom.
4. Perception of the partnership in context of the higher wisdom.
5. How does the partnership already work with the wisdom?
6. Where could the relationship improve according to this wisdom?
7. The relationship direction.

SHOULD I STAY OR SHOULD I GO?

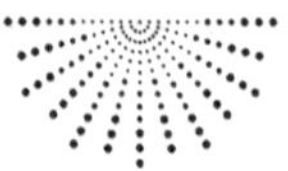

Many of us reach points in our relationships where we must seriously question the value of continuing with the union, or whether there is greater value in ending the relationship.

It is never an easy question, never a simple answer.

This deceptively simple spread provides a starting point for facing these tough situations.

You might find a satisfying answer, or at least enough to prompt further solo thought, by simply drawing the four cards. However, many find it useful to draw further clarifying cards for each of the following points. Be aware that the question "should I stay or should I go?" when we are in romantic relationships can be endless, so listen carefully to your intuition when to stop drawing clarifier cards.

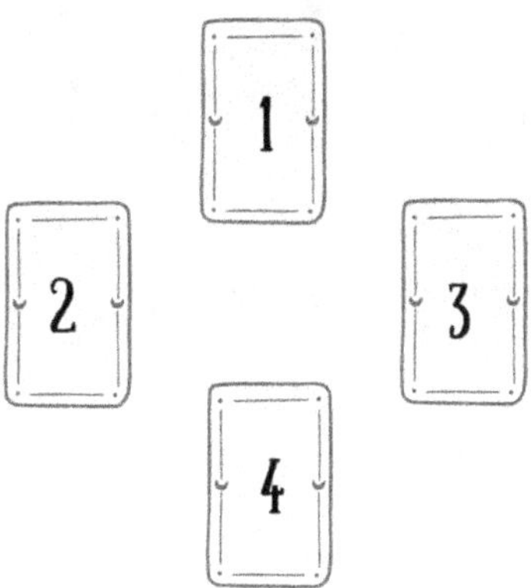

SHOULD I STAY OR SHOULD I GO?

1. The current state of the relationship.
2. Reasons for staying.
3. Reasons for leaving.
4. How to navigate the two to make the best choice.

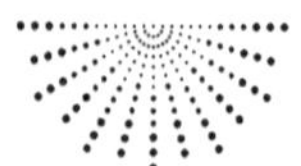

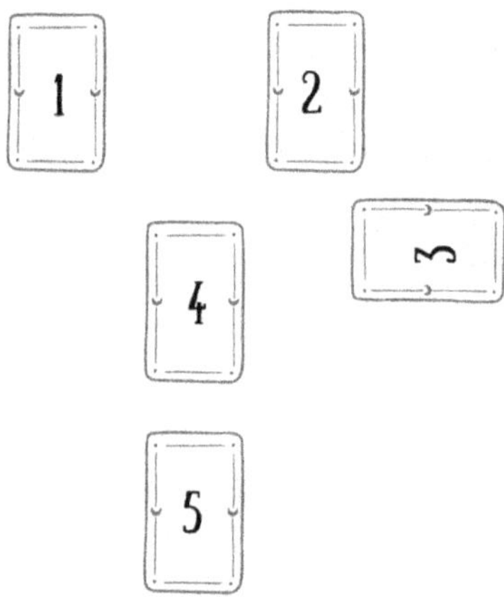

NAVIGATING ROUGH PATCHES

All relationships face inevitable challenges of one kind of another. Some hardships are simple, with defined edges and obvious paths to say on the roads. Others are endlessly complex and don't have definitive Yes/No, Best/Worst scenarios. This spread can work for either type of problem as it focuses on the positive nature of repair, in that there are usually things we can do to heal one another and strengthen our relationships. It isn't necessarily a "should we break up or should we stay together?" questioning, but can be used whenever the path gets rocky or hard to navigate.

1. Your role in the challenges.
2. Your partner's role in the challenges.
3. External influences beyond either's control.
4. Action you can individually take.
5. Outcomes.

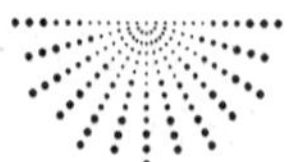

SEARCHING FOR LOVE

1. Why are you seeking love in a romantic partnership?
2. Ideal qualities of your future partner.
3. Your needs that must be met.
4. How to meet your new person.

5. Hidden obstacles already hindering your search.
6. Best thing to focus on about yourself right now,
    which has nothing to do with love or romance.

EMBRACING SINGLE LIFE

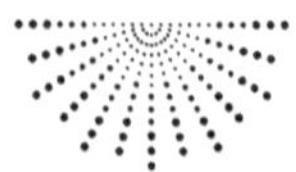

Singles are not always looking to change their relationship status. Despite the importance our culture places on forming romantic unions, if you are single, it is possible to enjoy single life and all the empowering benefits it can bring.

This isn't to say that by embracing the single life, you are cutting yourself off from the opportunity of being in a romantic relationship. It is about putting yourself, your own desires, your own fulfillment of your own path, ahead of the search for a romantic partner.

Embracing Single Life can be a potent spread to do following a break-up when you're just not ready, or just not interested in another partner.

1. Your present emotional state.
2. Personal growth opportunities.
3. Solo adventures and new experiences.
4. Ways to nurture individual passions and interests.
5. Your openness to the prospect of a romantic relationship.

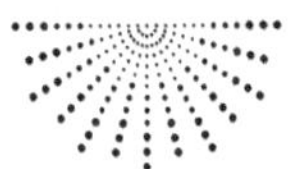

RELATIONSHIP TOUCHSTONE

The Relationship Touchstone is a check-in tool used to get an overview of what's going on in your partnership.

It doesn't have to be used during difficult times, but can also provide a lovely opportunity to check-in and strengthen what's already working really well.

The spread can be performed alone, reflecting on your

union solo. Alternatively, you may like to involve your partner either in examining the cards together, or have you each perform a separate spread and comparing and contrast in the individual results.

If you are performing the spread as one spread together, you might like to add additional cards to represent your individual selves in each card position.

1. Interpersonal Energy

Unveils the current energy dynamics of the pairing.

2. Authentic Feelings

Explores your genuine emotions and sentiments regarding your partner.

3. Experience Of Togetherness

The emotional landscape when you are together.

4. High Points Of The Relationship

The strongest fortifications of your connection.

5. The Primary Challenge

The most significant obstacle or challenge you are currently navigating as a partnership.

6. Your Partner's Needs

What your partner seeks from you.

7. Your Needs

What you want from your partner.

8. Furthering The Bond

Offers guidance on specific actions to enhance and fortify your connection.

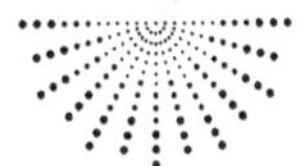

COMPATIBILITY

1. Your Significator.
2. Their Significator.
3. Your differences as a two unique individuals.
4. The common values and interests you two share.
5. Emotional compatibility.

6. Physical compatibility.
7. Spiritual compatibility.
8. Overall compatibility.

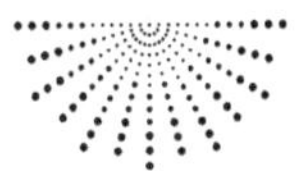

REPAIRING THE RELATIONSHIP

1. What do I want?
2. My needs aren't being met because...
3. My expectations aren't being met because...
4. Greatest point of conflict.
5. Hidden obstacle/s we both avoid.

6. Something to let go of.
7. A message from my higher self.

SHADOW AND LIGHT

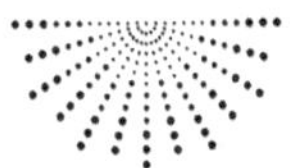

Every person is an interplay between shadow and light. This can be our strengths and weaknesses, our consciousness and subconsciousness. It can be our obvious dreams and our hidden desires.

The shadow doesn't have to be a negative aspect of our personalities. It is simply the parts of us which operate underneath our conscious awareness.

Since every person is made up of shadows and light, every relationship is going to be a complex interplay of shadow and light as well.

Often the shadows and lights of the relationship itself are entirely different from the shadows and lights of the individuals that make up the spirit of that union. This spread looks to what's in the shadows and light between a couple.

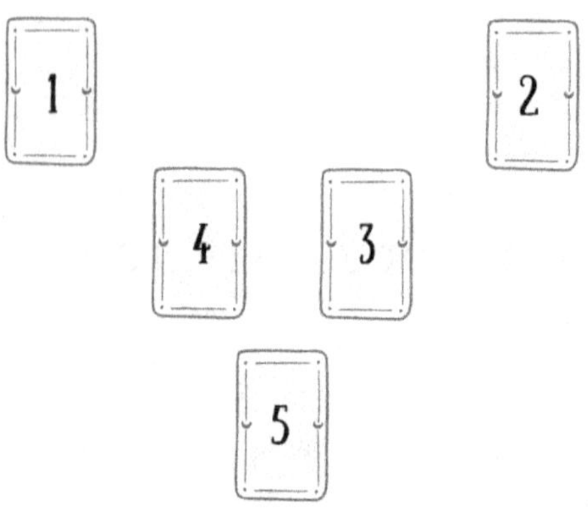

SHADOW AND LIGHT

1. Significator for you.
2. Significator for your partner.
3. What is in the shadows between you?
4. What is in the light?
5. How to illuminate the path forward.

THE THIRD WHEEL

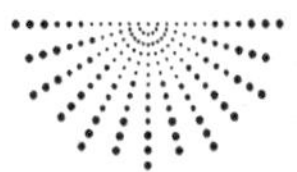

This spread helps to explore any third wheels affecting your relationship.

This might be in the form of another suitor, someone you suspect your partner is involved with, someone who is attempting a relationship with you, or someone you are looking outside your current relationship toward.

It is not always a potential affair you are looking to explore here. It might also be an influential family member, such as a parent-in-law, that is upsetting the balance in your relationship.

THE THIRD WHEEL

1. Significator for me.
2. Significator for my partner.
3. Significator for the relationship.
4. Significator for the third wheel.
5. Challenges the third wheel brings.
6. Path to overcome the challenge.

GETTING BACK TOGETHER

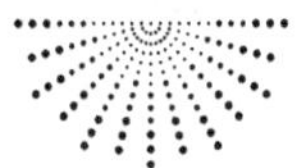

If you've ended a relationship and are looking at that former partner with fresh eyes, this spread can provide a touchstone for your thinking if getting back together with them might be the best idea.

1. The biggest challenge to your potential reunion.
2. Your perception of your ex's sentiments about you.
3. The most probable outcome.

IN LOVE WITH THE LAW OF ATTRACTION

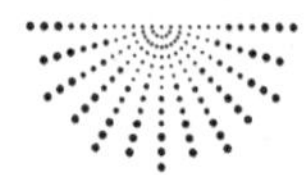

The Law of Attraction is a belief system based on the idea that the energy we emit into the universe through our thoughts, feelings, and beliefs influences what we attract into our lives.

Advocates of the Law of Attraction believe that, by focusing on positive thoughts and emotions, individuals can manifest their desires and achieve their goals. Conversely, dwelling on negative thoughts may attract unwanted experiences or outcomes.

The Law of Attraction is often associated with practices such as visualization, affirmations, and maintaining a positive mindset to align one's thoughts and desires with their intended outcomes.

This spread looks at certain ideals of the Law of Attraction in relation to bringing more romantic love into your life.

IN LOVE WITH THE LAW OF ATTRACTION

1. Limiting beliefs that are preventing you from fully embracing love.
2. Aspects of your mindset that need adjusting to attract a loving connection.
3. Practices you can adopt to cultivate a more loving and open-hearted approach.
4. How you are unintentionally repelling love.
5. How you can amplify your allure.
6. Next action you need to take to align yourself with the energy of love.

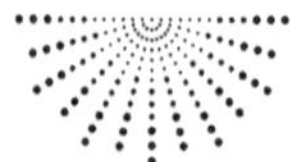

WHERE IS MY LOVER?

1. Why haven't I encountered the love of my life so far?
2. What steps can I take to draw them into my life?
3. What preparations should I make to be ready for their arrival?

4. How will I recognize when I've found the love of
    my life?
5. Where is the most likely place for me to encounter
    them?
6. What factors need to come together before I cross
    paths with the love of my life?

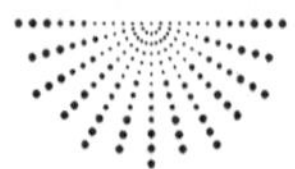

GROWING TOWARD LOVING UNIONS

1. How can I strengthen my ability to trust others?
2. In what ways can I enhance my commitment in relationships?
3. What simple steps can I take to improve my communication skills?

4. How can I practice being more open and vulnerable in my interactions?
5. What aspects of self-reflection will contribute to finding lasting love?
6. Are there specific patterns in my behavior that may hinder trust, and how can I address them?
7. What daily habits can I adopt to foster a more trusting and committed mindset?
8. How can I express my emotions more effectively to build stronger connections?
9. What role does self-love play in establishing lasting and fulfilling relationships?

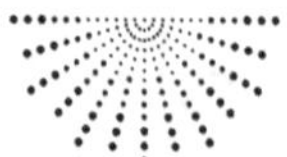

The Celtic Cross is a traditional, ten card tarot spread, often used to give a broad analysis of a circumstance. Alternatively, it can be used as a deep dive into one aspect of the situation.

When interpreted with a focus on love and romance, each position of the Celtic Cross can provide insights into different aspects of your love life or a specific relationship.

The position labels of this spread vary from reader to reader, although there's a general similarity for the Celtic Cross used by most readers.

The labels I've used here are slightly different to the Celtic Crosses I've written about in other books, aiming to provide a unique spin for matters of love.

1. The Present

This card represents either the current state of your love life, or you in general, if you have not drawn a separate Significator card.

2. Positive Forces

Strengths in your romantic life. If a negative card is drawn, consider this a block against potential positive forces.

3. Higher Wisdom

A message from your higher self, or divine spirit.

4. Subconscious

Ways your subconscious is filtering into your conscious life, revealing your true thoughts, feelings, and aspirations.

5. The Foundation

The roots of your romantic situation, including all past events that color the present union.

6. All Relationships

The state of your relationships overall, not just your romantic unions.

7. Yourself

Your psychological state in the context of your romantic situation.

8. Your Environment
External factors or influences that affect your love life.

9. Hopes and Fears
Your innermost desires and fears regarding your romantic life.

10. Outcome
The potential outcome of your love situation.

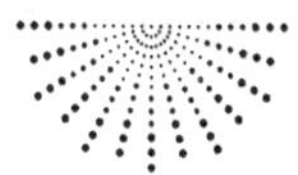

The Horseshoe Spread is a frequently used tarot spread, useful for wide-ranging overviews on various aspects of life. I've adapted it here for a specific focus on love and relationships.

1. Current Relationship

The current state of your love life or an existing relationship.

2. What Crosses You
Challenges or obstacles affecting your love life.

3. Recent Past
Insights into recent events or experiences that have influenced your romantic situation.

4. Near Future
What may unfold in your romantic life in the near future.

5. Self-Perception
Your thoughts and feelings about your role in the relationship.

6. Partner's Perspective
Your partner's thoughts, feelings, or actions in the relationship.

7. Advice
How to navigate challenges and enhance the positive aspects of your love life.

8. External Influences
External factors that may be affecting your relationship.

9. Hopes and Fears
Your hopes and fears regarding your love life, and life in general.

10. Outcome
The potential outcome of your romantic situation.

YOUR CORE EMOTIONAL NEEDS

Each of us has a series of core emotional needs that psychologists believe need to be met in order to be a contented and fulfilled human.

This spread delves into the psychological theories of our core needs and provides a holistic view of your emotional fulfillment.

1. Security and Stability
How generally secure you are in getting your most basic human needs met. This includes things like housing, nutrition, and other basic services.

2. Connection and Relationships
How you connect and form relationships with others.

3. Autonomy and Independence
How much you are able to be yourself within your relationships.

4. Expression
How well can you express your inner worlds? This might be

in formal creative pursuits like writing or art, or just through day to day living.

5. External Recognition and Validation
How you are seen and validated by those around you in an emotional sense.

6. Inner Fulfillment
How whole do you feel considering all the above?

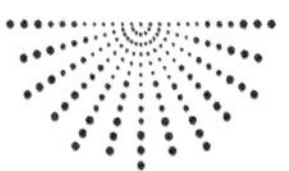

ROMANTIC ATTACHMENT

This spread is designed to provide insight into the dynamics of attachment theory psychology in the context of romance, fostering self-awareness, and offering guidance for healthier connections.

Basically, attachment theory is about how we form bonds with people in our lives. It starts with our caregivers in infancy, extends to friendships, and is deeply enmeshed in romantic unions.

There are many valuable books written on attachment theory in relationships, if you are not already familiar with this concept. You might like to brush up on what attachment styles are before reading this spread, and get an idea of what your personal attachment style would be categorized as.

1. Your Attachment Style Overview
Reveals your current attachment style in relationships.

2. Early Influences
Explores the influence of early experiences on your attachment style in adult romantic relationships.

3. Communication Dynamics
How your communication style may be influenced by your attachment style, and the effect this has on your romantic connections.

4. Fear of Abandonment
Conscious or unconscious fears related to abandonment and how they manifest in your romantic relationships.

5. Intimacy and Vulnerability
How comfortable are you with intimacy, emotionally and physically?

6. Security Building Blocks
Actions you can take to build a sense of security within your romantic relationships.

REKINDLING THE FLAME

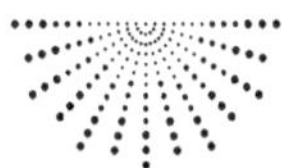

All relationships go through ebbs and flows of intensity, and a low burning moment need not mean the ultimate end of your love.

If you're in a period where your warmth isn't burning as brightly as you would like, use this spread to rekindle your flame.

1. Current Disconnect
The current aspects of your life where you feel a disconnect from your lover.

2. Past Influences
What events or experiences have shaped your relationship so far?

3. Your Partner's Feelings
Your lover's feelings toward this low point.

4. Inspired Action
What practical steps can you take to spark up your passion?

TAROT SPREADS FOR SELF-LOVE

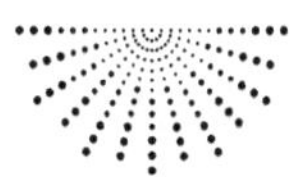

10 SINGLE CARD DRAWS FOR SELF-LOVE

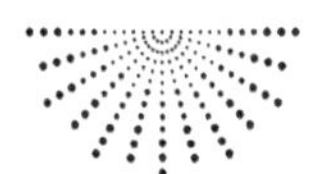

You might like to use these single card topics to direct a daily draw ritual, or consult them whenever you need guidance in any of the given areas.

You might like to do one card over ten days and then, at the end, look at the ten cards as a unified spread and see what you can discern about your overall state of self-love.

1. Acceptance
How to embrace all aspects of yourself without judgment or reservation.

2. Compassion
How to extend kindness, empathy, and understanding towards yourself.

3. Forgiveness
The act of releasing past grievances and self-blame, allowing space for healing, growth, and inner freedom.

4. Gratitude
How to cultivate an appreciation and thankfulness for your

experiences, blessings, and journey in order to foster a sense of abundance and contentment.

5. Boundaries

Steps towards establishing healthy limits, protecting your needs, values, and personal space.

6. Nurturing

How to best practice self-care, prioritizing your well-being and growth on physical, emotional, and spiritual levels.

7. Empowerment

Your personal strengths and inner resources available to pursue goals, assert boundaries, and navigate life's challenges.

8. Authenticity

How you can be free to express your true thoughts, feelings, and desires without fear of judgment or rejection.

9. Joy

Ways you can embrace moments of happiness, pleasure, and fulfillment, in order to celebrate life's beauty and find delight in everyday experiences.

10. Balance

How to pursue equilibrium and harmony in various aspects of life, including work, relationships, self-care, and personal growth.

DAILY SELF-REFLECTION RITUAL

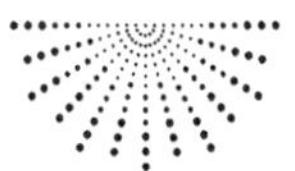

A daily single card draw is a gentle self-care ritual that invites many opportunities for self-reflection.

It's easy. At the start of each day, draw a single card.

This practice invites the card's positive energy into your day, or directs your attention to aspects of yourself that may benefit from nurturing.

You might also like to keep a journal to reflect on your interpretations and notice any recurring themes or insights that emerge. At the end of each week, look back on your daily cards. What themes do you notice?

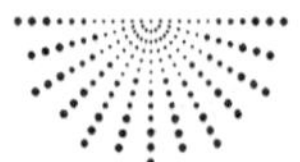

SELF-LOVE OVERVIEW

1. You currently.
2. Your inner strengths and other positive qualities.
3. Hidden positive aspects of yourself.
4. Current challenges or barriers hindering your self-love journey.

5. Areas requiring self-acceptance.
6. Positive external forces and influences.
7. Boundaries with others.
8. Areas to practice more vulnerability.

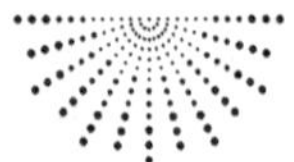

HONORING MYSELF

1. How can I recognize and appreciate my true worth?
2. In what ways can I demonstrate to myself that I deserve value?
3. What obstacles prevent me from making my own needs a priority?

4. What insights does my higher self have to share
   with me?
5. What is my self-perception like?
6. In what manner can I express my genuine self?
7. What must I let go of to fully embrace and accept
   who I am?

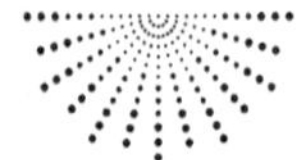

I LOVE MYSELF

Sometimes it's hard to say "I love you" in any relationship. It's even harder for most of us to say it to ourselves. Much of the time, we aren't conditioned to express love for ourself in such overt ways, but learning to actively express self-love in this simple yet profound statement can open the doors to enormous opportunities for growth.

This spread helps you to get into your feelings about yourself so that you might more easily say to yourself, "I love you."

1. Current limiting beliefs about myself.
2. How I share my gifts with myself.
3. Obstacles to eliminate on the path to "I Love Me."
4. Expressions of self-love I already do.
5. My authentic self.

THE TIME TRAVELING SELF

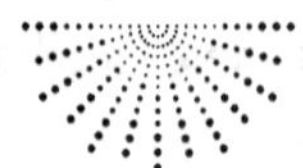

1. What does my inner child need?
2. What does my future self need?
3. What does my present self need?

THE PATH TO SELF-CONFIDENCE

1. My talents.
2. Positive qualities I don't see about myself.
3. Something to release.
4. The pathway to confidence.

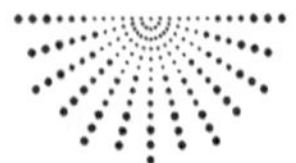

PRACTICAL SELF-LOVE

1. Your most loveable quality (in your own eyes).
2. How you show yourself kindness.
3. How you are hurtful to yourself.
4. What to let go of.
5. The next right thing.

FRIENDSHIP

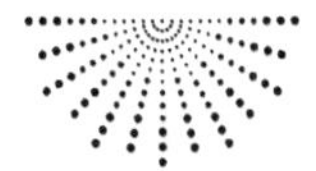

10 SINGLE CARD DRAWS FOR FRIENDSHIP

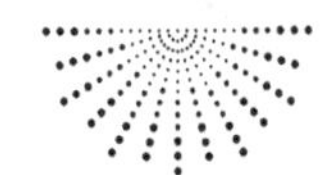

If you've got matters of friendship on your mind, and you are looking to consult the cards for a quick, powerful shot of wisdom, here are ten themes through which to explore friendships with single card draws.

To perform a deep overview spread, draw cards for these themes and use them in a single epic spread together. You might like to do this over ten days, seeing what emerges at the end of a series of daily draws.

1. Gratitude
Being grateful for the friends in your life and the positive aspects they bring.

2. Supportive Energies
How your friends are supporting you and how you support them.

3. Communication
Communication within your friendships.

4. New Connections

Potentials for new friendships or connections.

5. Shared Joy
How do you share moments of joy and happiness with your friends?

6. Understanding
How well you and your friends understand each other on a deeper level.

7. Challenges
Challenges in your friendships.

8. Quality Time
The nature of the quality time you spend with your friends.

9. Appreciation
Appreciating the unique qualities and contributions of each friend in your life, and you in theirs.

10. Boundaries
How to set healthy boundaries in your friendships for mutual respect and understanding.

EXPLORING FRIENDSHIP DYNAMICS

Like any relationship, friendships can get complicated. The love we share with a friend differs from the love we have with a romantic partner or a family member, but is no less impactful. There are different dynamics at play in friendships, different expectations of how the relationship serves each person.

Use the spread to get an overview of your friendship dynamics either in times of struggle, or even if things are going smoothly.

1. Current State of Friendship
What is the foundation of your connection right now?

2. Shared Memories
What shared moments have shaped your friendship?

3. Emotional Connection
How do you and your friend connect on a deeper, emotional level?

4. Challenges
Factors causing tension or difficulties in the present or past.

5. Strengths of the Friendship
What qualities or elements contribute to the bond you share?

6. Unspoken Feelings
What may be hidden beneath the surface?

7. Advice
What steps can you take to strengthen your connection?

8. Potential Changes
What transformations might be on the horizon?

9. Future of the Friendship
The forward path of your relationship.

FORMING FOUNDATIONAL FRIENDSHIPS

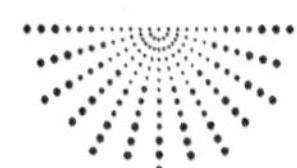

Not all friendships are the same. Some are closer, some are just for fun, some step only just outside of the bounds of acquaintances. Other friendships, rare bonds, go to the core of everything we are. I call these foundational friendships.

If there is a person you connect with, and would like to advance that relationship, use this spread to think about how your relationship could support a deeper emotional connection and become a foundational friendship.

1. Mutual Understanding
How well do you and your friend understand each other?

2. Support and Trust
How strong is the foundation of trust, and how do you support each other?

3. Potential Growth
What opportunities exist for the relationship to deepen and develop over time?

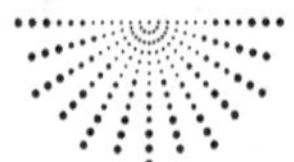

MAKING NEW FRIENDS

Adults often find it hard to make new friends. It might be because we are too busy in our day to day lives to widen our social circles and meet new people. Maybe we're too entrenched in ourselves, in our views, in our social positioning to even know how to let new people in.

This spread can be used if you're looking to bring new friends into your life, but you're not sure where to start.

1. Current Social Circumstances

What is the backdrop against which you'll be seeking new friendships?

2. Personal Readiness

What aspects of yourself are you bringing into potential new connections?

3. Qualities to Seek in Friends

What attributes do you desire in a friend?

4. Opportunities for Connection

Where might you find like-minded individuals and potential friends?

5. Overcoming Barriers

What obstacles might you need to overcome to connect with others?

6. Future Friendships

What can you expect as a result of your efforts in seeking new connections?

STRENGTHENING FRIENDSHIPS

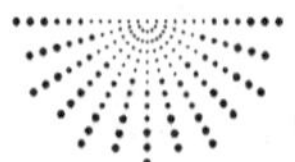

Just like romantic relationships, friendships need work. Sometimes that work is to strengthen the bond, or it might be to repair faults and move forward together into a more rewarding relationship for the both of you.

1. Current Strengths
What positive qualities or dynamics contribute to the love between you and your friend?

2. Areas Needing Attention
Where can you focus your efforts to enhance the connection?

3. Communication Enhancement
How can you improve the way you and your friend communicate to deepen your bond?

4. Shared Activities
What activities can you engage in together to foster a stronger connection?

5. Future Growth

What can you do to ensure continued growth and deepening of the love between you and your friend?

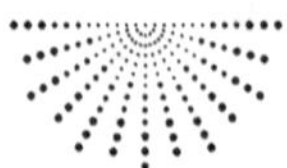

REPAIRING FRIENDSHIPS

Falling out with friends can be just as emotionally damaging as breaking up with a lover.

Most of us have friends who come and go through our lives. That's normal and natural. However, this spread refers more to when you have had a specific breakdown with your

friend that you would like to repair, reconnect, and grow
from.

1. Previous state of the friendship.
2. The friendship after the rupture.
3. Root cause of discord.
4. Communication breakdown.
5. Paths to reconciliation.
6. Future harmony.

PARENT AND CHILD LOVE

10 SINGLE CARD DRAWS FOR PARENT-CHILD RELATIONSHIPS

Here are ten key themes of parent-child relationships to explore through single card draws.

If you're wanting a more thorough exploration of your parental relationships, draw cards for each of these themes and incorporate them into a unified, expansive spread.

1. Nurturing Connection
Explore the current environment of nurturing and emotional connection between the parent and child.

2. Generational Wisdom
Reflect on the wisdom and lessons passed down through generations within the family.

3. Empathy and Understanding
Focus on the level of empathy and understanding present in the parent-child relationship.

4. Supportive Guidance
Consider the guidance and support provided by the parent to the child in various aspects of life.

5. Communication Harmony

Explore the harmony and effectiveness of communication between parent and child.

6. Expressing Affection

Reflect on how affection and love are openly expressed and received within the family.

7. Balancing Independence

Consider the balance between fostering the child's independence and maintaining a supportive connection.

8. Creating Memories

Explore how the parent and child create lasting and cherished memories together.

9. Respecting Differences

Focus on the mutual respect and acceptance of individual differences within the parent-child relationship.

10. Teaching and Learning

Reflect on the ongoing process of teaching and learning that occurs between the parent and child.

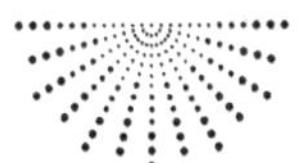

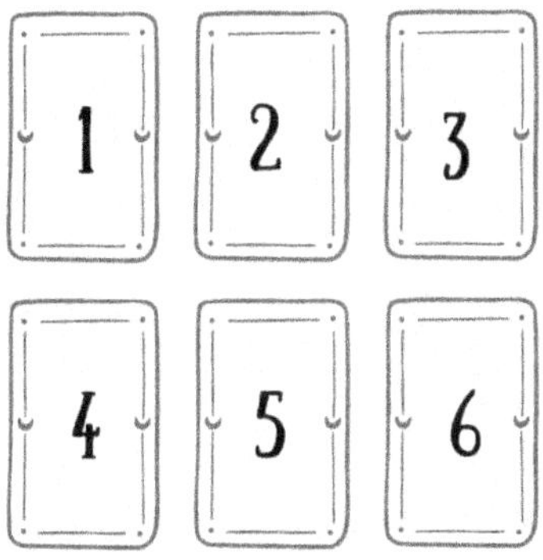

CONNECTING WITH YOUR CHILDREN

This spread aims to deepen understanding and strengthen the bond between parent and child, promoting a loving and supportive relationship. It can be used when times are tough and you're experiencing discord in your relationship, or it can be used at any time to get insight into the general relationship. The ideas here can be used with young children and adult children.

1. Love Foundation
Reveals the current foundation of love between you and your child, showcasing the strengths and areas for growth.

2. Understanding and Empathy
Explores your understanding of your child's emotions and needs, emphasizing empathy as a crucial component of your relationship.

3. Communication Harmony
Examines the quality of communication between you and your child, highlighting areas of connection and potential improvement.

4. Support and Nurture
The ways in which you provide support and nurturing to your child, addressing their emotional and practical needs.

5. Shared Joyful Moments
Celebrates the positive and joyful moments you and your child share, fostering a sense of connection and happiness.

6. Growing
Provides insights into the potential growth and evolution of your love and connection with your child in the future.

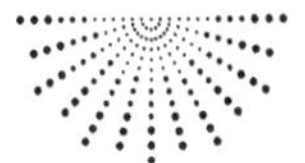

PARENTAL GROWTH

In order to grow and thrive, any relationship requires growth on both sides. In a child and parent relationship, the child is naturally developing into their adult self. But, in order to do this with their best chance at reaching their potential, children need loving guidance and modeling from parents. This seems obvious and simple, but for many

parents, it's incredibly hard to put into practice as they themselves have not been shown how to grow and actualize their
full potential.

This spread looks at areas where a parent might need to
focus on their own growth in order to help a child fully
thrive.

1. Parent's Influence

Qualities and energies the parent brings into the
relationship.

2. Child's Influence

Qualities and energies the child contributes to the relationship.

3. Love Expression

Ways in which love is communicated within the relationship
from parent to child.

4. Challenges

Potential challenges or obstacles in the parent-child relationship.

5. Emotional Empathy

How well emotions are understood and navigated within the
relationship.

6. Parental Growth

Main area where the parent needs to focus on growth in
order to support and guide the emotional growth of the
child.

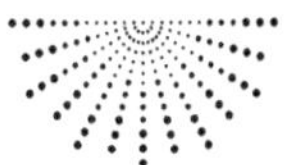

CONNECTING TO A PARENT

The spread has been designed from the perspective of an older child (an adult or an older teen), to help explore their relationship with their parents in order to either reconnect or strengthen their bond.

1. Core

Foundational aspects of the relationship between you and
your parent, from your perspective.

2. Communication
How effectively are you communicating with your parent?

3. Emotional Empathy
How well do you understand your parent's emotional
situation?

4. Challenges
The major challenges or obstacles hindering your relationship.

5. Strengths
The strengths and positive aspects of your relationship.

6. Growing Up
The potential for growth and transformation on both sides
within your relationship.

THE CHILD GUIDE TO LOVE

Some of the greatest life lessons a parent can learn come directly from their children. This spread asks you to think about the bond you share with your child, how it manifests inside of the both of you, and what you can learn from your child's innocent perspective.

1. Cherished Memories
Significant events or experiences that hold sentimental value.

2. Nurturing Growth
How your love nurtures your child's as well as your own personal and emotional growth.

3. Parent's Guidance
Wisdom and influence you bring to your child's life.

4. Child's Past Advice
What your child has already taught you.

5. Child's New Wisdom

Something you're yet to learn that your child is already showing you.

HEALING BETWEEN PARENT AND CHILD

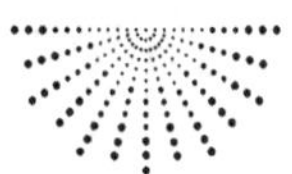

1. Healing Energy
2. Past Wounds
3. Current Nurturing
4. Open Communication

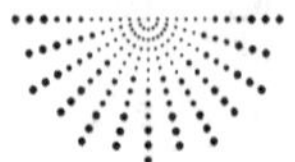

ALL IN THE FAMILY

This is a spread designed to get an overview of the entire family, with multiple children and multiple parents.

It can apply to all family units, whether that is a single or multi-parent family, same-sex parents, one child, many children, blended families, and any other form a family can take.

Gendered terms "paternal" and "maternal" have been used to represent the ends of the energy spectrum these parental roles operate within, not the gender or sex of a particular parent. For example, a woman can express paternal strength (masculine/animus), and a man can express maternal nurturing (feminine/anima). Please apply your own labels if these don't feel right to you and your family dynamic.

1. Paternal Strength

The positive paternal strength and support within the family unit.

2. Maternal Nurturing

The positive maternal nurturing aspects of the group.

3. Inherited Traits

Dominant inherited traits and qualities passed down from parent/s to child/ren.

4. Emotional Bonds

Nature of the emotional bonds shared between the parent/s and child/ren.

5. Guidance and Mentorship

The guiding and mentoring role of the parent/s in the child/ren's life.

6. Mutual Respect

Mutual respect between parents and children.

7. Celebrating Differences

Positive acceptance and celebration of the differences between parent/s and child/ren.

8. Languages of Love

The ways love is expressed within the family unit.

9. Legacy of Love

The lasting legacy of love between the generations.

DIVINE LOVE

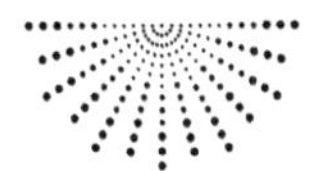

A NOTE ON GOD

When I refer to God in this chapter, I employ the label as simply one word many people use to identify their understanding of the divine source energy. I am not specifically referring to a Christian god or any other deity specific to any religion, spiritual belief or practice.

Other common terms are the divine, source, deities, the universe, spirit, essence, and there are many others. You might have your own special words. Please use whatever term fits best with your experience and understanding of the essential force of creation.

10 SINGLE CARD DRAWS FOR YOUR RELATIONSHIP WITH DIVINE SPIRIT

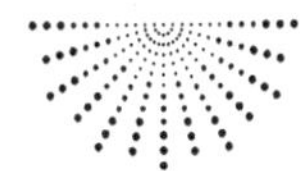

The following is a list of ten themes for single card tarot draws intended to help you explore your relationship with the spirit forces in your life.

If you're wanting a more thorough exploration of your relationship with your divine, draw cards for each of these themes and incorporate them into a unified, expansive spread. This could be done over ten days, meditating every day on the day's theme.

1. Faith and Trust
The trust you have in your relationship with the divine. How can you deepen your trust in the guidance and presence of the divine spirit?

2. Surrender
How do you surrender to your divine?

3. Guidance
The guidance you are receiving from the divine spirit.

4. Connection

The current state of your connection with the divine. How can you strengthen this connection?

5. Love
How can you open your heart to receive and express more divine love in your life?

6. Communication
The channels of communication between you and the divine.

7. Gratitude
What aspects of your life or experiences are you grateful to the divine for?

8. Patience
Aspects of your life that require patience and trust in divine timing?

9. Divine Presence
Your level of awareness of the divine presence in your daily life. What can you do to become more conscious of the divine's presence and guidance throughout your day?

10. Resistance
In what ways are you resisting a divine presence in your life?

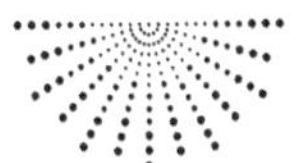

This spread aims to provide insights into one's spiritual connection, devotion, and the path towards a deeper understanding of divine love.

1. Foundation of Faith
The foundation of your spiritual connection with God.

2. Influences of Faith

What aspects of your faith are currently influencing your understanding of divine love?

3. Current Devotion

How are you currently expressing your love and devotion towards the divine?

4. Blessings Received

Reflect on the blessings and grace that you have received on your spiritual journey.

5. Obstacles to Devotion

Any obstacles or challenges hindering the flow of divine love in your life.

6. Divine Guidance

Current guidance you are receiving from the divine.

7. Spiritual Growth

Ways you can continue to grow in your understanding and experience of God's love.

THE HEART'S PATH

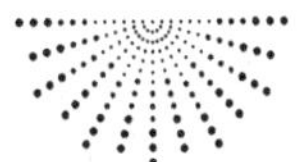

1. Heart Connection

What emotions and feelings are present in your relationship with your God spirit?

2. Divine Guidance

What messages or guidance is the divine offering to enhance your connection?

3. Path of Devotion

Explore the path of devotion laid out before you.

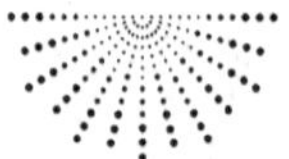

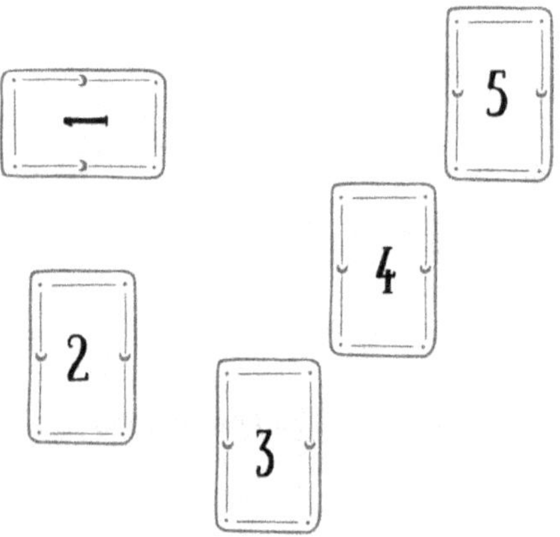

RECONNECTING WITH GOD

If you have lost your way on your spiritual path, you might look to rekindle your relationship with your divine spirit. Use this spread to understand how you fell from your path and to also recognize how God is already calling you back into a loving connection.

1. Current Disconnect

The current aspects of your life where you feel disconnected from the love of God.

2. Past Influences

What events or experiences have shaped your relationship with the divine?

3. Divine Invitation

This card symbolizes the invitation from the divine to reconnect.

4. Inspired Action

What practical and spiritual steps can you implement to strengthen your bond?

5. Divine Assistance

What energies or assistance is God providing to aid you in rediscovering divine love?

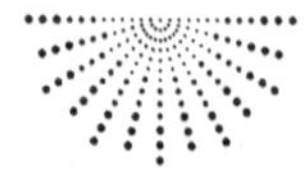

EXPLORING A MUTUAL BOND WITH THE DIVINE

1. Your Spiritual Essence
2. Divine Qualities
3. Communication With Spirit
4. Challenges
5. Spiritual Growth Opportunities
6. Mutual Creation

CONNECTING TO THE UNIVERSE

1. Current Spiritual State
2. Your Inner Guidance
3. Sacred Practices
4. Tests of Faith
5. Surrender To Faith
6. A Divine Message

MORE BOOKS ON TAROT BY KAT ELMWOOD

Tarot For Beginners

Tarot For Money

Yes No Tarot

Tarot Meanings

For More Tarot Resources Go To

www.tarotjunction.com

ABOUT THE AUTHOR

Kat Elmwood (she/her) is a lifelong tarot devotee.

Kat has practiced tarot for over thirty years and has had a deck on hand for every life stage.

She is an author in multiple genres (fiction and nonfiction) under multiple pennames, an artist, a mother, and many other titles.

Kat's current favorite tarot deck is *The Wandering Star Tarot* by Cat Pierce.